Child's Own Book of Great Musicians

Original works by Thomas Tapper
compiled by RaeAnna Goss

THIS BOOK BELONGS TO:

Timothy   Farrer

HOW THIS BOOK WORKS

This book is meant to be individual to each child studying the composers. Activities within the book include cutting and pasting images while learning more about the great musicians. Tapper's individual composer books are available for free in the public domain, however the time it takes to format and print for the intended use potentially causes too much valuable time for the average homeschool mom or teacher! Not to mention the cost of paper and ink! This convenient printing and curating provided through this book allows students to open and go with the composer studies for the year.

Simply cut on the dotted line and allow students to cut and paste into the book! Image numbers are added to make it easy to find where they belong in the story. Have fun! Glue sticks or double sided tape are recommended over liquid glue paste.

TO THE STUDENT

You are about to read and discover more about the lives of Johann Sebastian Bach, Wolfgang Amadeus Mozart, and Ludwig Von Beethoven! Three of the most influential composers of our western classical music traditions! I hope that you will enjoy listening to recordings by these great masters and continue learning more about their music and passions. Learning fun facts like how many kids Bach had, how young Mozart was when he could compose music, and how Beethoven could still write music even after losing his hearing brings about a personal connection to these masterful composers!
Have fun reading and listening!

-RaeAnna Goss

TABLE OF CONTENTS

Bach 1685-1750   **Mozart 1756-1791**   **Beethoven 1770-1827**

BACH

The Story of the Boy Who Sang in the Streets

This is the house in which JOHANN SEBASTIAN BACH was born. (image 1)

This house stands in the town of Eisenach in Germany. It looks very much the same today as it did when Sebastian was a little boy. Many people go there to visit this house because the little boy grew to be a famous man.

In Eisenach there is a statue of Bach near the palace. (image 2)

In the same town in which Sebastian was born there stands on the top of a hill a very famous castle built many hundreds of years ago.

This castle is called the Wartburg. (image 3)

As a boy little Sebastian used to climb the hill with his friends, and they, no doubt, had a happy time playing about the castle grounds. In one of its great halls the minstrels of Germany held their Song Contests.

When Sebastian was old enough he used to travel afoot, just as the minstrels did; his purpose was to go to hear fine organ players. Once as he sat weary by the roadside someone threw a herring to him so that he might eat as he rested. (image 4)

Little Sebastian's father was named JOHANN AMBROSIUS BACH. He, too, was a musician, as his people had been for many years. (image 5)

One of these was a miller who played and sang while the corn was grinding. His name was Veit Bach, and his little boy was called Hans, the Player, because he, too, loved to play the violin. (image 6)

When Sebastian was ten years old his father and mother died. So he went to live with his brother, whose home was a few miles away.

Of this brother Sebastian had music lessons, and he improved so rapidly that he used to beg to be allowed to play the pieces in a big book in the library.

But the brother refused him this pleasure. However, little Sebastian was eager to learn all the music he could find, so he used to sit up on moonlight nights and copy these pages while his brother was asleep.

But what do you think happened when he had copied everything in that big book?

His brother found out what he had done and took all his precious music away from him. (image 7)

If you know any boy who is about twenty years old you may say to him, Bach was as old as you are when Benjamin Franklin was born in Boston.

And although there was this difference of twenty years or so in their ages, we may think of them at work in the world at the same time. You must remember that all men like Franklin and Bach who became famous did so by working very hard. (image 8)

BENJAMIN FRANKLIN.

Franklin, too, was born very poor. Once he walked the streets of Philadelphia with a loaf of bread under each arm. But by being faithful in all he did he became the friend of all his countrymen and of Kings and Queens besides.

Benjamin Franklin was quite a little younger than Sebastian Bach. But there was a famous man who was almost exactly Sebastian's age. This man composed an Oratorio that is loved by everybody. It is sung in cities and towns all over the world, particularly at Christmas time.

Do you happen to know the name of this Oratorio? If not, you can surely learn it by asking someone or by looking it up in a book.

The Oratorio, the name of which you have just written, was first sung in the Irish city of Dublin, 1742. (image 9)

At that time Sebastian Bach was living in Leipzig and had been for many years at the head of the Thomas School. He was known as its Cantor. Bach worked very hard here to supply music for several of the Leipzig churches, and he worked so well that his fame spread until it reached the ears of the Emperor.

Frederick the Great was also a musician and composer. So he invited Sebastian Bach to visit him at his castle. There were many people present, but Sebastian Bach was the principal guest. He played on many of the Emperor's fine pianos.

When he reached home again he composed a musical work and dedicated it to the Emperor. (image 10)

BACH PLAYING BEFORE FREDERICK THE GREAT.

The kind of a piano that Sebastian Bach played on was not called a piano in his day. It was called a Clavier or Clavichord.

Some day you will study a collection of pieces by Sebastian Bach which was written for this instrument and was called The Well Tempered Clavichord.

This is the kind of piano, or clavichord, that Bach used. (image 11)

THE CLAVICHORD

And here is the beginning of the very first piece in the collection of which we have just spoken in Bach's handwriting. (image 12)

Sebastian Bach had a very large family, twenty children altogether. Two of them studied music faithfully with their father. (image 13)

MORNING PRAYERS IN THE HOME OF JOHANN SEBASTIAN BACH

One was Friedmann, for whom the father wrote a book called Little Preludes. Friedmann's brother, Philipp Emanuel Bach, was a very fine clavichord player. He wrote a book about music and composed many pieces. (images 14 and 15)

WILLIAM FRIEDMANN BACH.

PHILIPP EMANUEL BACH.

Sebastian Bach died in 1750. He was sixty-five years of age.

Benjamin Franklin was at that time forty-four years old and George Washington was eighteen.

This is the way Bach wrote his name. (image 16)

SOME QUESTIONS.

1. In what year did Bach die?
2. Name an American who was alive at the same time.
3. What famous castle can be seen from the streets of Eisenach?
4. What other great German composer lived in Bach's time?
5. What instruments could Bach play?
6. For what purpose did Bach travel from place to place, as a boy?
7. What was the name of Sebastian's father?
8. Who was Hans, the Player?
9. Were any of Bach's children musical?
10. What music by Bach have you heard?

THIS PAGE INTENTIONALLY LEFT BLANK.

MOZART

The Story of a Little Boy and His Sister Who Gave Concerts

The composer whom we call WOLFGANG AMADEUS MOZART was
called Wolferl when he was a little boy. He had a sister, MARIA ANNA,
who was called NANNERL. Nannerl was five years older than her brother.
She had lessons from her father on a kind of piano called a harpsichord.
Here is a picture of one. (image 1)

When Wolferl was three years old he used to listen to Nannerl's playing. He
always watched and listened when Papa Mozart gave her a harpsichord
lesson. Little as he was, he would often go to the harpsichord and try to pick
out tunes with his chubby fingers. His father noticed that Wolferl could
remember quite a little of the music that Nannerl was practising.
And here is a picture of Wolferl trying to reach the keys so as to play the
melody of his sister's lesson. (image 2)

When Wolferl was four years old he began to take lessons.

While he practised no one ever spoke to him because he was so serious about it. If other children came to play with Nannerl he would make music for their games and marching; playing in strict time all the while.

Here is Nannerl's picture when she grew up to be a young lady. (image 3)

Father Mozart loved both of his children deeply and often played with them. The violin was the instrument he liked best and little Mozart had daily lessons in his home. Here we see him playing while his sister sings. (image 4)

In this picture we see Papa Mozart, who was a very fine player on the violin. Wolferl and Nannerl are playing the piano. (image 5)

When Wolferl was nearly six his father took him and Nannerl on a concert tour. Everybody wanted to hear them play and they gave many concerts.

Wolferl spent all his boyhood with his music. He went to many places to play, even as far from Salzburg, in Austria (where he was born), as to Paris and London.

Everywhere he went people were happy to see him and his sister and to hear them play. And they, too, were happy to play because they loved the music so much.

When they reached Vienna they played for the Emperor and Empress.

When Wolferl was presented to the Empress he jumped up into her lap and kissed her.

Wolferl was always busy composing music. But he played games and had a good time just like any other boy. When he was busy with his music, however, he never let his thoughts go to anything else.

But we must not go too fast, for we want to see how Wolferl is growing up.

Here is his picture when he was five years old and beside it another when he was eight years old. Do you see his wig and sword? (image 6 and 7)

MOZART AT FIVE.

Everybody in Paris wanted to hear Wolferl play when they knew that he had come, so they asked him to read at sight; to play the bass part to a melody and to accompany a song without seeing the music.

People also took great delight in asking him to play on the harpsichord with a cloth stretched over the keyboard so that he could not see the keys.

They all went to London to play for the King. The King wanted to see for himself how skilful little Mozart was, so he gave him pieces by Bach and Handel to play at sight. Mozart read them off at once. Here is a fine picture of the Mozart children when they played for the King and the Queen. (image 8)

MOZART AT THE COURT OF THE EMPEROR.

It must have been very fine for a little boy of seven to play for kings and queens. But Wolferl was not spoiled by it all. He was just a happy hearted boy all the time.

He always made it a rule to put his mind on what he was doing and do it the very best he knew how.

It is just as good a rule now as it was when he was alive.

It is time now that we learned the birthday of Mozart. If we think of it every year on the 27th of January, it will be easy to remember it.

In what year was he born?

Here is another picture of Mozart in 1766. How old was he then? (Beethoven was born four years afterward.) (image 9)

MOZART IN 1766.

When anyone is always busy at one thing he soon gets a lot done. As Wolferl grew and kept on writing music all the time he made a great many pieces. Some were short like a song, others were long like an opera. He wrote for the piano, the violin and the voice. And he composed operas, symphonies and ever so many other kinds of music.

Mozart liked to be alone when he was working upon his compositions. He used to go to a little house on the edge of Vienna and lock himself in.

The people of the city of Salzburg, in Austria, took this house long after Mozart's death and moved it to a park where all may go to see it, just as we in America go to see the houses of William Penn, Lincoln and Washington. (image 10)

WHERE MOZART COMPOSED.

Can you remember, without turning back, the year in which Mozart was born?

Some other great musicians were alive at that time. And during his lifetime some were born who became great men.

In the year when Mozart was born both Handel and Haydn were living. And Haydn lived eighteen years after Mozart's death.

You can remember it by these lines: (image 11)

1732	The years of Haydn's life	1809
	1756 The years of Mozart's life 1791	

When Mozart was fourteen years old Beethoven was born. Mozart knew him and he knew Papa Haydn also, and they were very good friends.

In our own country there lived in Mozart's lifetime Benjamin Franklin and three Presidents of the United States—George Washington, John Adams and Thomas Jefferson.

I wonder if Washington ever heard of Mozart?

Perhaps we can best keep all these names together by looking at this page now and again.

1706   Benjamin Franklin was born.
1732   Washington and Haydn were born.
1736   Patrick Henry was born.
1743   Thomas Jefferson was born.
1750   Bach died.
1756   WOLFGANG AMADEUS MOZART was born.
1759   Handel died
1770   Beethoven was born.
1771   Walter Scott was born.
1790   Franklin died.
1791   Mozart died.
1809   Joseph Haydn died.

Isn't it fine to think of Mozart writing so much music, so many operas, symphonies and sonatas; traveling so much, meeting so many people and never being spoiled by it all.

While he wrote many very great pieces of music, here is something he composed when he was five years old. He made up the pieces at the piano and his father wrote them down note for note in a little copy book. (image 12)

SOME QUESTIONS.

1. In what country was Mozart born?
2. In what city was Mozart born?
3. Where did Mozart play before the Emperor and the Empress?
4. Did Mozart play games and have a good time like other boys?
5. Why did people ask Mozart to play upon the harpsichord with a cloth stretched over the keys?
6. Whose compositions did the King of England ask Mozart to play?
7. What great American patriot was born in the same year as Haydn?
8. Which lived the longer life, Haydn or Mozart?
9. Have you ever heard a piece by Mozart?
10. Was Mozart spoiled by meeting many people?

BEETHOVEN

The Story of a Little Boy Who Was Forced to Practice

Ludwig van Beethoven was born in the lovely town of Bonn, on the River Rhine, December 16, 1770.

The house in which he spent his boyhood is still standing. We see in the picture what a pretty, homelike place the house and the yard must have been. It is now the Beethoven House, or Museum, filled with mementos of the great composer. There you may see music pages written by him, letters, medals, instruments; even his ear trumpet is there. (image 1)

Beethoven's father was a singer at the Chapel of the Elector. He was not a good father, for he did not care to work even enough to make his family comfortable. But the mother loved her boy with all her heart, as we shall see. (image 2)

THE BEETHOVEN HOUSE

BEETHOVEN'S FATHER

Ludwig was only four years old when he began to study music. Like children of to-day he shed many a tear over the first lessons. In the beginning his father taught him piano and violin, and forced him to practice. At school he learned, just as we do to-day, reading, writing, arithmetic, and later on, Latin. (image 3)

THE FIRST LESSON

Never again after thirteen, did Ludwig go to school for he had to work and earn his living.

Do you wonder what kind of a boy he was?

We are told that he was shy and quiet. He talked little and took no interest in the games that his boy and girl companions played.

While Ludwig was in school he played at a concert for the first time. He was then eight years old. Two years later he had composed quite a number of pieces. One of these was printed. It was called Variations on Dressler's March. On the title page of this piece it said:—

VARIATIONS ON DRESSLER'S MARCH
Composed by a Young Amateur
LOUIS VAN BEETHOVEN
Aged ten years. 1780

Then the little boy studied with a teacher named Christian Gottlob Neefe, who took real interest in him. Neefe did not, as was said of Beethoven's father, punish the little boy severely to keep him at his practice, hour after hour.

Often when Neefe had to travel Ludwig took his teacher's place as organist at the Court. Then with the organ lessons there were other lessons in Harmony. So rapidly did the boy improve that his teacher said one day:

"If he goes on as he has begun, he will some day be a second Mozart."

Our young hero of thirteen was surely busy every hour of the day. He played in an orchestra, as accompanist. He gave lessons, played the organ in church, studied the violin, and kept up his work in composition. He always kept a note-book for musical ideas.

Most every child in these days has more and better opportunities than had the great Beethoven when he was a child. Here is a picture of the funny old organ in the Minorite Church of Bonn upon which Beethoven played when he was a little boy. (image 4)

BEETHOVEN'S ORGAN

Look at the funny stops at the top and compare it with the best organ in your own town. This is little better than a toy beside our fine organs of to-day,— yet it was the best that Beethoven had to practice upon. When Neefe said that he would probably be a second Mozart the words filled Ludwig with a great desire. On his sixteenth birthday what do you think happened? Why, he set out from Bonn to Vienna, where Mozart lived.

But scarcely had he begun to feel at home in Vienna when news came to him that his mother was ill. She had always been a good mother, kind of heart, great of hope for her little boy, and probably she sympathized with the hard lot that made him have to work so early in life. When he learned of her sickness he hastened to Bonn.

Who was happier, he said to one of his friends, than I, so long as I was able to speak the sweet name of Mother and know that she heard me? (image 5)

BEETHOVEN'S MOTHER

Vienna had given him a wonderful happiness. He met Mozart and had some lessons from him in composition. When he played for the great master, Mozart tip-toed from the room and said softly to those present:

"Pay heed to this boy. He will surely make a noise in the world some day." (image 6)

BEETHOVEN AND MOZART

After his Mother's death he determined that he would remain there. And it was not until he talked with Joseph Haydn, who stopped at Bonn on his way to London, that he decided once more to journey to Vienna. Beethoven was twenty-two years old at the time he met Papa Haydn. Beethoven showed the master some of his compositions. Haydn urged him to go at once to Vienna, promising to give him lessons in composition on his return from London. (image 7)

JOSEPH HAYDN

Everywhere in Vienna Beethoven was a welcome guest. He was proud (but in the right way), very honest, always straightforward and independent. But, like his mother, he was warm-hearted and as true as could be. There was nothing in his nature that was mean, or cruel, or wrong in any way. He took pride in his talent and worked hard to perfect himself in it.

Here is what Beethoven's handwriting looked like. (image 8)

BEETHOVEN'S HANDWRITING

Bit by bit, the great power of Beethoven as a pianist became known. He played much among his friends, but he did not like to perform in public.

A story is told that once he was to play his C major Concerto at a concert. When he arrived at the hall he found the piano was tuned so low that he had to play the Concerto in C# major.

You know how hard it is to transpose a simple piece, but think of transposing a Concerto and playing it with orchestra without time for practice!

Do you sometimes wonder what the great composer looked like? Beethoven lived outside of Vienna and often took long walks in the country. Once a little boy ten years of age was taken by his father to visit Beethoven. The boy must have been a very observant boy for he wrote out a description of how Beethoven looked. This is the little boy's picture as a man: (image 9)

CARL CZERNY

And this is the description he gave of Beethoven.

"Beethoven was dressed in a dark gray jacket and trousers of some long-haired material, which reminded me of the description of Robinson Crusoe I had just been reading. The jet-black hair stood upright on his head. A beard, unshaven for several days, made still darker his naturally swarthy face. I noticed also, with a child's quick perception, that he had cotton wool which seemed to have been dipped in some yellow fluid in both ears. His hands were covered with hair, and the fingers were very broad, especially at the tips."

You know, of course, that when we think of music we think of hearing it. We think how it sounds to us. A lover of music loves to hear its tones and to feel its rhythm.

Like every other human being, Beethoven loved music in just this way. He loved its sounds as they fell on the ear. As colors delight our eyes, so tones fell with delight upon the ears of this man.

Beethoven was once invited to play at the home of a nobleman, but upon being informed that he would be expected to go as a menial, he indignantly rejected the proposal. (image 10)

THE ANGRY BEETHOVEN

Beethoven had many friends and was fond of them. They knew that he was a genius and were glad to forget some of the very strange things that he did when he got angry. Here is a picture of the great master seated among a group of his friends. Although Beethoven was odd, his friends loved him. (image 11)

But a strange Fate touched him and took away his sense of hearing. From the time he was about thirty years old his hearing grew gradually worse. Indeed it was necessary for him to have a piano especially constructed with additional wires so that he could hear. (image 12)

BEETHOVEN PLAYING FOR HIS FRIENDS

BEETHOVEN'S PIANO

Can you think of anything more cruel, more terrible, more depressing, more awful? (image 13)

BEETHOVEN IN THE COUNTRY

And yet he went on day, after day, composing beautiful music as he walked the fields, or as he sat at his table. For we must remember that he could hear his own music in his thoughts. That is, the mind that made the music could hear it, though the ear itself was forever closed to the sound of it.

Year after year he continued to write symphonies and concertos, sonatas, songs, choral and chamber music.

And year after year the poor ears closed a little more and still a little more, until finally not even the loudest noises could penetrate them.

And yet he worked bravely; writing every beautiful music thought that came to him, so that the world, and that means you and all of us, might have them. When Beethoven was dying in 1827, Schubert called upon him and remained with him for some time. (image 14)

BEETHOVEN AND SCHUBERT

SOME QUESTIONS

1. When and where was Beethoven born?
2. Who was his first teacher?
3. What did his father do?
4. How long did little Ludwig go to school?
5. What description of him as a boy in school has been given?
6. How old was he when he first played in public?
7. What composition of his was first to be published?
8. Which of his teachers took great interest in him?
9. What did he say about the little boy's future?
10. Where did Beethoven go when he was sixteen years old?
11. With what two great masters did he study?
12. What composer, as a little boy, went to see Beethoven?
13. How did he describe him?
14. Name some of the forms of music which Beethoven composed.
15. Write a list of music by Beethoven that you have heard.
16. What is a concerto? a sonata?
17. How old was Beethoven when he died?